The Deeper Things of God Series • Book One

THE PERSONAGE OF GOD

*An In-depth Look at the Godhead-Trinity
Known of as Elohim . . .
That Hebrew Declaration to Which the Three Persons
Known of as God The Father, and God The Son,
and God The Holy Spirit Belong to.*

Robert E. Daley

The Larry Czerwonka Company, LLC
Hilo, Hawai'i

Copyright © 2015 by Robert E. Daley

All rights reserved. No part of this book may be reproduced or transmitted in any form or by any means, electronic or mechanical, including photocopying, recording or by any information storage and retrieval system, without written permission from the author and the publisher.
For information email info@thelarryczerwonkacompany.com

First Edition — March 2015

This book is set in 14-point Garamond

Published by: The Larry Czerwonka Company, LLC
http://larryczerwonkapublishing.com

Printed in the United States of America

ISBN: 0692383832
ISBN-13: 978-0692383834

All scriptures used in this work are taken from the
King James Version of the Scriptures.

BOOKS BY **ROBERT E. DALEY**

A Case for "Threes"
A Simple Plan . . . of Immense Complexity
Armour, Weapons, And Warfare
from Everlasting to Everlasting
Killer Sex
Life or Death, Heaven or Hell, You Choose!
Raptures and Resurrections
Short Tales
So . . . What Happens to the Package?
Study and Interpretation of The Scriptures Made Simple
Surviving Destruction as A Human Being
The Gospel of John
The Gospel of John (Red Edition)
The League of The Immortals
The New Testament - Pauline Revelation
The New Testament - Pauline Revelation Companion
"The World That Then Was . . ." & The Genesis That Now Is
What Color Are You?
What Makes A Christian Flaky?
What Really Happened to Judas Iscariot?
Who YOU Are in Christ . . . RIGHT NOW!

The Enhancement Series

    #1 Book of Ecclesiastes
    #2 Book of Daniel
    #3 Book of Romans
    #4 Book of Galatians
    #5 Book of Hebrews

The Deeper Things of God Series

    #1 The Personage of God
    #2 The Personage of Man
    #3 The Personage of Christ

Contents

The Immutability of Counsel **1**

The Study of God **8**

Before the Beginning **11**

In the Beginning **21**

The Creation of Man **37**

The Personage of The Father **41**

The Personage of The Son **51**

The Personage of The Holy Spirit **68**

THE PERSONAGE
OF GOD

The Immutibility of Counsel

Within a gospel tract written by a man named Winkie Pratney, who is associated with the Last Day Ministries in Lindale, Texas, the mathematical precision of the Scripture is demonstrated through the work of a young Russian Harvard graduate named Ivan Panin, which was begun by Mr. Panin in 1882. Mr. Pratney's presentation is quite impressive and impacting. He goes on to say:

"The whole Bible is like this. I am just taking one small chunk of it and doing it in detail. Every paragraph, passage and book in the Bible can be shown to be constructed in the same marvelous way. What kind of fantastic collaboration between the disciples could have produced this structure without computers? How could mere fishermen and tax-collectors produce this kind of incredible structuring and design? What is crazy is that Mark is a Roman, Luke a Greek, and Matthew a Jew, but they all wrote with the same pattern. Each one wrote with their own unique flavor. Mark's style is different, but the pattern is the same right through! So who wrote it? One Mind, one Author . . . one God . . . many different writers, but one Writer. Can you imagine what kind of Mind would do this and not even care if you ever found out? What I want you to see is

how smart God is! These are not just words, it's an incredible mathematical pattern. It dances with its own poetry in mathematics. A computer would go into raptures over this! It's like a building where every piece joins perfectly with each other. And what is wild, is you can't pull even **one** *word out, without damaging the whole pattern. So the Bible carries within itself, a self-checking, self-verifying protection factor. If a person comes along and says I don't like this one, the whole pattern falls apart. This cannot be found in any other religious 'holy' book in the world."*

* * *

On March 20, 1969, at a meeting of the Pediatric Society, a man named Dr. Richard L. Day . . . who had been an instruction professor since 1935 . . . and had just finished his term as National Medical Director of Planned Parenthood . . . and was currently a professor of pediatrics at the Mount Sinai School of Medicine . . . and who was considered an *insider* within something called **The Order** was quoted as saying:

"You will forget most or much of what I am going to tell you tonight . . . the old religions will have to go . . . especially Christianity. Then a new religion can be accepted for use all over the world. It will incorporate something from all of the old religions to make it more easy for people to accept and feel at home. Most of the people will not be too concerned with religion. They will

realize that they do not really need it.

In order to do this, the **Bible** *will be changed. It will be rewritten to fit the new religion.*

Gradually, **key words** *will be replaced with new words having various shades of meaning.*

Then the meaning attached to the new word, can be close to the meaning of the old word . . . and as time goes on, other shades of meaning for that word, can be emphasized . . . and then gradually that word replaced with another word.

The few who do notice the difference will not be enough to matter . . . And, the churches will help us!"

It was stated that the idea within this calculated assault upon the Word of God, is that everything within the Scripture does not need to be rewritten . . . just certain **key words** to be replaced by other words.

The variability in meaning attached to any word can be used as a tool to change the **entire** meaning of the Scripture, and, therefore, make it acceptable to this *new* religion. Most of the people will not even know the difference.

It was also stated that Dr. Day was concerned that if what he had stated within that relaxed atmosphere ever really became known, that his days would be numbered.

Within just a few months of informational release, Dr. Day was dead.

* * *

The whole of this study of The Deeper Things of God finds its basis within the unchanging Word of God, utilizing only the King James Version Translation of the Bible . . . and no other translation version will be acceptable for use within this study.

* * *

The supreme authority on the subject of God . . . is God Himself. He has granted unto us *"**all things** that pertain unto life and godliness, through the knowledge of him that hath called us to glory and virtue."* (II Peter 1:3b)

Jesus of Nazareth said, *"**Sanctify them through thy truth: thy word is truth.**"* (John 17:17)

For this reason, we will rely totally upon the written Word of God and upon the Word-of-God-supported Holy Spirit revelation, in the presenting of spiritual truth and existence realities. The Word of God itself testifies:

*"**The Law of the Lord is perfect, converting the soul: the testimony of the Lord is sure, making wise the simple.***

The statutes of the Lord are right, rejoicing the

heart: the commandment of the Lord is pure, enlightening the eyes.

The fear of the Lord is clean, enduring for ever: the judgments of the Lord are true and righteous altogether.

More to be desired are they than gold, yea, than much fine gold: sweeter also than honey and the honeycomb.

Moreover by them is thy servant warned: and in keeping of them there is great reward." (Psalms 19:7-11)

* * *

"To the law and to the testimony: if they speak not according to this word, it is because there is no light in them." (Isaiah 8:20)

* * *

"So shall my word be that goeth forth out of my mouth: it shall not return unto me void, but it shall accomplish that which I please, and it shall prosper in the thing whereto I sent it." (Isaiah 55:11)

* * *

"For the word of God is quick, and powerful, and sharper than any two-edged sword, piercing even

to the dividing asunder of soul and spirit, and of the joints and marrow, and is a discerner of the thoughts and intents of the heart." *(Hebrews 4:12)*

* * *

"Wherein God, willing more abundantly to show unto the heirs of promise the immutability of his counsel, confirmed it by an oath:

That by two immutable things, in which it was impossible for God to lie, we might have a strong consolation, who have fled for refuge to lay hold upon the hope set before us." *(Hebrews 6:17-18)*

* * *

"We have also a more sure word of prophecy; whereunto ye do well that ye take heed, as unto a light that shineth in a dark place, until the day dawn, and the day-star arise in your hearts:

Knowing this first, that no prophecy of the Scripture is of any private interpretation.

For the prophecy came not in old time by the will of man: but holy men of God spake as they were moved by the Holy Ghost." *(II Peter 1:21)*

* * *

The testimony of the Word of God applies to every subject or situation that we may encounter. The Word of God is our foundation . . . the Word of God is the bottom line . . . the Word of God is the end of the story . . . the Word of God is what God is. Everything that we will be looking at within our studies will find its foundation within the Word of God.

The Study of God

The *New Webster's Dictionary* defines:

Theology *noun*
1) the study of God and the relations between God and the universe.
2) a study of religious doctrines and matters of divinity.
3) a specific form or system of this study, as expounded by a particular religion or denomination.

Systematic Theology *adjective*
1) a determined, calculated, in-depth, orderly study of that Being within this universe known of as God.

Being *noun*
1) existence, one who exists.

Being *adjective*
1) (in the phrase) for the time being; for the present.

Person *noun*
1) a man, woman, or child, regarded as having a distinct individuality or personality, or as distinguished from an animal or a thing.

In person
1) being physically present.

Ergo . . .
(A **being**, as referring to a person, is one who exists . . . one who is. One who is tangible and real, having substance. A **person**, is a being who is regarded as having a distinct individuality or personality.)

God is not an Idea. He is not an Essence. He is not a Concept. He is not an Aspect. He is a real Person. All Three Members of the Godhead are real Persons.

Within the context of our study, it is our desire to consider, and take a comprehensive look at the Being of, and the Personage of God . . . and to cultivate and develop a more defined fellowship with each Person.

* * *

The immutable counsel of the Word of God declares that:

"God is a Spirit: and they that worship him must worship him in spirit and in truth." *(John 4:24)*

From the testimony of the Spirit of Truth, we are informed that God is indeed a real Being. He is, in fact, a real spirit Being. He is indeed a real, *infinite*, spirit Being . . . which means that He is beyond natural or supernatural limitations.

Man, on the other hand, is a *finite* being . . . which means that he is restricted by natural and supernatural limitations.

A *finite* being **cannot** fully comprehend the *infinite* Being because there is no common point of reference to measure from, within the everlasting contexts that exists.

Before the Beginning

Before the beginning... God is.
NOTHING precedes God: Nothing comes before God. Nothing exists before God.

There is no *Beginning* before God.
There is no *Time* before God.
There is no *Creation* before God.

Existence is... but The Personage of God is the totality of all *Existence*.

ILLUSTRATIVELY speaking for the benefit of our simple brains... on a standard blank sheet of white paper... on the extreme left-hand side of the page... halfway down, in the middle of the page... place a large ¼" black dot. This dot will be used *illustratively* to represent God.

To the left-hand side of that dot, there is NOTHING. Above that dot, there is NOTHING. Below that dot, there is NOTHING. And to the right-hand side of that dot there is NOTHING.

The Personage of God is... but there is NOTHING else.

* * *

"Through faith we understand that the worlds were framed by the word of God, so that things

which are seen were not made of things which do appear." (Hebrews 11:3)

"For the <u>invisible things</u> of him from the creation of the world are clearly seen, being understood by the things that are made, even his eternal power and <u>Godhead</u>; so that they are without excuse:" (Romans 1:20)

So what **invisible things** might we be able to understand concerning decisions and actions that were most assuredly taken by the Members of the **Godhead** at this point?

1) Since within the One God Godhead there are Three Members . . . a decision needs to be amicably arrived at, concerning who will occupy the equality Position number One . . . and who will occupy the equality Position number Two . . . and who will occupy the equality Position number Three.

2) Since by Divine design there shall be three different full and active operational Realms of Existence brought forth . . . emanating directly from the very God which is the **fullness** of existence . . . a decision needs to be amicably arrived at, concerning the

operational order of those Three Realms . . . and who will be the Head of, and Administrator of, each particular Realm of *Thought*, *Word*, and *Deed*.

3) Since by Divine design, and because of granted free-will moral agency, there shall be three valid **States of Being** for moral creation to reside in . . . those designated conditions need to become established, manifest, and secured even before one free-will moral creature is brought forth. Those States of Being include . . . the **State of Being *Immortal***, which is the reality of being untouchable by any of the aspects of death when it comes forth . . . and the **State of Being *Eternal***, which is the reality of having the capacity to live forever if continued obedience is chosen . . . and the **State of Being *Mortal***, which is the reality of being death-doomed without reprieve.

4) Since within the One God Godhead there shall be various responsibilities and task-assignments that shall need to be performed by each of the Three Members . . . several decisions need to be amicably arrived at

concerning who will handle and then be held accountable for various specific tasks.

And it must further be agreed upon that no One Member will cross-over any of the designated lines of separated-task-assignment responsibilities.

5) Since the Three Members of the One God Godhead are not at all confused or befuddled concerning who they are . . . but Mankind, when it is brought forth, is certain to be unclear concerning who is actually who . . . titles and names need to be amicably arrived at for each of the Three Members according to their assigned responsibilities.

6) Since the aspect of free-will decision for all of moral creation shall become the centermost issue within all of Existence . . . and since Divine Foreknowledge *(Isaiah 46:10)* is already aware of the two major rebellions that shall come forth within the two Probationary Periods that will occur . . . there needs to be the drafting of two specific Plans of Redemption and Reconciliation that shall be made available for acceptance to *whosoever* requires them. The Plan of Redemption is

designed for *Mankind*, which requires the application and usage of the physical element of Blood for ratification . . . and a Plan of Reconciliation is designed for all *Angelic Hosts* and all *Other Creatures*, which does not require the usage of the Blood element.

7) When we understand that there are restoration opportunities that shall be provided for broken relationships, we should also understand that a set of accurate records needs to be prepared and preserved for *fairness* purposes. There shall be a single *Book of Life* prepared for the accurate name preservation of every single Express Image creature of the Living God that exists among the constituency of *Mankind* (Hebrews 1:3) who has chosen the path of life-everlasting through Jesus Christ of Nazareth. And there shall be prepared, a set of other *Books* that contain accurate record-keeping of all errant activities of moral creation run amok. (Revelation 20:12)

8) A superior project of divine design that within the process of *Time* will actually deal with an unprecedented creation of a new species of moral being, shall be prophetically

drafted in liquid silver and dipped in transparent gold by the creative hand of predestination. *(Romans 8:29)* All of the details concerning this project are fully completed and in order even before one-second of created *Time* ticks by. Everything having to do with this particular project is finished ahead of *Time* because the whole of this project is accomplished by the full Personage of God through the future God/Man, and for the benefit of the New Creation new-species constituents that shall be birthed into it. Simple belief and acceptance of what God has done is the initial requirement for entrance. *(John 6:29)* Willful continued obedience and adherence to regulation mandates will fully seal the *off the charts* benefits that go with this plan. *(Revelation 17:14)*

9) Since God is a Creator and not a magician, of necessity the creation-regulation-restrictions . . . or the creative laws by which all things shall be brought forth into existence, and then operate by, need to be drafted, established, and installed. This includes the initial base-set of laws (both spiritual and natural) and also whatsoever associate supportive

laws that might apply that will work harmoniously and cooperatively with those base-set of laws.

*   *   *

ILLUSTRATIVELY speaking for the benefit of our simple brains . . . take the same blank sheet of white paper . . . and one-quarter of an inch directly to the right-hand side of the first established ¼" black dot that *illustratively* represents God . . . put a second ¼" black dot of the same size.

This second black dot *illustratively* represents the creation of the element of *TIME*. From the very center of that second dot, draw a line at a forty-five degree angle in an upward direction to the right. Then from the very center of that second dot, draw a line at a forty-five degree angle in a downward direction to the right. The wedge that is created *illustratively* represents the very beginning of the created element of *TIME*, and the continuum or corridor or time-net . . . into which all *things* that shall then come forth may be creatively placed into.

* The created element of *TIME* is an **Existence Gauge of Measurement.**

TIME has been integrated by God respectively into seconds, minutes, hours, days, weeks, months, years, decades, centuries, and millennia.

TIME is not suspended, nor interrupted, nor stopped for anything. Any activities, or situations, or issues that are occurring within operational *TIME* may be changed . . . but *TIME* itself is static and unalterable.

The Personage of God has come from without the element of *TIME*, in order to create and establish the element of *TIME*, and then He has encapsulated Himself within the operational parameters of *TIME*.

Speaking of that which is called *dateless* . . . without the element of *TIME* there is not even the potential of any date, let alone anything that may be considered *dateless*.

The Sun, and the Moon, and the Stars, do not direct or cause *TIME* to function . . . *TIME* itself functions indepentantly, and the Sun, Moon, and Stars are gauged and adjusted to operate within the *TIME* parameters.

TIME has been broken down into three basic segments for understanding and clarity.

Yesterday . . . which is <u>*expired-TIME*</u> that has already past . . . and all that has transpired within that *TIME*-past cannot be altered or revisited. Once it was the vapor of vision. And it has since stepped over the threshold from the thence into the now, and run its course. Now it has dissipated, and moved on unto expiration.

Today . . . which is current *operational-TIME* . . . is that in which decisions can be made, faith can be released, creative words can be spoken, and future hopes can be drafted. It took a great while for it to arrive, and it shall be gone before we are really able to get our hands wrapped around it. Today is the one substance of *TIME* that we can lay hold of. This narrow envelope slice of *TIME* carries stupendous potential. Today we have the opportunity to speak those things which be not as though they were. *(Romans 4:17)*

Tomorrow . . . is *expected-TIME* that yet resides within the future. Even now, tomorrow is too far away to see clearly. Tomorrow can be anticipated, but is not able to be grasped. It is elusive. Anxiety is nervously waiting for tomorrow to dawn. Fear is crouching at the door, awaiting daybreak. Dreams live within the realm of tomorrow. Days of anticipation are all lined-up and waiting for their turn to step through the doorway of tomorrow.

Please note that from that first illustrative creative black dot, representing *TIME* origin . . . there is no *Time Volume* to the left within our diagram whatsoever. However, there is a tremendous amount of *Time Volume* exponentially to the right of that black dot.

The consistently ticking element of *TIME* is now irreversibly in existence. The Beginning has Begun . . .

ordered steps of creation can now take place . . . from this beginning point there will now be no opportunity afforded to go *Back to the Drawing Board*.

In the Beginning

ILLUSTRATIVELY speaking for the benefit of our simple brains . . . take the same blank sheet of white paper . . . and one-quarter of an inch directly to the right-hand side of the second ¼" black dot that *illustratively* represents the element of *TIME* . . . put a third ¼" black dot of the same size. This third ¼" black dot represents the initiation of Creation.

1) The first ordered step of creation within the collective net of *time* is the releasing from the very Personage of God, and then the securement thereof, of all of the Three Realms of Existence. Those Three Realms become manifest even before there is any activity taking place within them.

   The primary Realm of Existence becomes the Realm of Thought. The First Person of the Godhead . . . He who today is known of within creation as **The Father** . . . is the agreed upon Supreme Regent of this whole universe. And, He is installed as the Head of and the Administrator of the Existence Realm of Thought. This is the origin Realm of the whole of the three existing Realms. All of the words that are spoken or the actions that are performed first stem from what originally initiates within the Existence Realm of Thought. *(Proverbs 23:7)* All thought activity even within the Godhead initially emanates forth from **The Father** by mutual agreement.

The secondary Realm of Existence becomes the Realm of Word. The Second Person of the Godhead . . . He who today is known of within creation as **The Son** . . . is installed as the Head of and the Administrator of the Existence Realm of Word. Words are innately constructive . . . words carry power . . . words can create . . . words are like building blocks. If you take the right number and the right kind of building blocks, and you interface them together correctly, they construct that which is desired, and bring into manifestation what was originally thought. Words that are not spoken are not really words at all, they are all still only thoughts. Words will set thoughts into motion.

"**All things were made by <u>words</u>; and without <u>words</u> was not any thing made that was made.**" *(John 1:3)*

In a practical application:

Thought activity gently flows forth from the First Person of the Godhead to the Second Person of the Godhead . . . and the Second Person of the Godhead drinks-in that thought activity, and chooses which precise words shall accurately express the flow of that thought, and appropriately approves those words that shall then be spoken.

A creatively secondary and actual Third Realm of Existence becomes the Realm of Deed. The Third Person of the Godhead . . . He who today is known of within creation as **The Holy Spirit** . . . is installed as the Head of and the Administrator of the Existence Realm of Deed. He is the agreed upon *power-portion* of the Godhead. He is the One who will *make it all happen.*

In a practical application:

Thought activity gently flows forth from the First Person of the Godhead to the Second Person of the Godhead . . . and the Second Person of the Godhead drinks-in that thought activity, and chooses which precise words shall accurately express the flow of that thought, and appropriately approves those words that shall then be spoken . . . *and the Third Person of the Godhead receives the precise spoken words that have been approved and whispered, and utilizes the creative laws that have been established to formulate things within the locale of the spiritual and then manifest them through the creative portal into the locale of the natural. And all of this activity can transition in less than one microsecond. "Things that are not, spoken of as if they were, are manifest forth into existence within the natural."* (Romans 4:17)

As a **must-know** post-script to these truths: All Three Members of the Godhead are absolutely equal . . . *in every respect*. All Three Persons can *think the same thoughts* . . . All Three Persons can *say the same words* . . . And all Three Persons can *do the same things*. They are inequitably-absolutely equal. Within Their operating harmony They simply do not always think the same thoughts, nor speak the same words, nor do the same things . . . <u>*at the same time*</u>. And that is the key! That is the *only* way that you can have Three Persons working so seamlessly and harmoniously together *as if* they were seemingly only One Person.

2) The second ordered step of creation within the collective net of *time* would be the bringing forth of the Spoken-Thought physical elements of Air, Water, Soil, and Fire . . . the first three elements of which are constructive, and infused with the decreed-creative-power of the Holy Spirit of God. These first three realities would become known of as the *Basic Creation Elements*, and would provide the very building blocks of imparted *life* to the inanimate flora and fauna portion of creation.

3) The third ordered step of creation within the collective net of *time* would be the initiating decrees of active operations concerning the actual formation of this universe. Divine purpose . . . mixed with elements of calculated balance are released through Spoken-Thought . . . and harmoniously combined with the *Basic Creation Elements* . . . and active formation and operations of the universe begin to take place.

> ***"For he spake, and it was done; he commanded, and it stood fast."*** *(Psalms 33:9)*

> ***"Then said the Lord unto me, Thou hast well seen: for I will hasten my word to perform it."*** *(Jeremiah 1:12)*

Because of what God has declared above, it can be reasonably determined that there is no possibility of any accurate *Time* calculation that can be attributed to or connected to universal formation and development, despite the projections of sin affected, two-dimensional-declared postulations that are put forth by men who continue to walk in darkness. The fact of the matter is that we are so much closer to *The Beginning* than is normally recognized or acknowledged, particularly within Christendom.

* * *

The Word of God declares that there are three created **Heavens**. *(II Corinthians 12:2) The First Heaven would be the atmosphere surrounding this planet Earth. The Third Heaven would be the operational headquarters and dwelling locale of God. And the Second Heaven would be all of the area in between and around the First and the Third Heavens.*

It is this *Second Heaven* that we are speaking about concerning the initial coming forth of within creation . . . inclusive of a universal creative order. The *Second Heaven* is the first one of the three heavens that was created.

* * *

4) The fourth step of ordered creation within the collective net of *time* would be the infusion of *Life* into the inanimate. As galaxies are formed, and solar systems are established, and planetary order is confirmed over incalculable *time* . . . where potential habitation is initially deemed acceptable, the *Basic Creation Elements* are utilized to establish a prophetical bubble for moral creation to be brought forth into the collective net of *time* and exist.

5) The fifth step of ordered creation within the collective net of *time* would be the initial creation of free-will, moral beings.

Of necessity, a determined "Probationary Period" is required with any free-will, moral agency. The created creature . . . over expired time . . . must demonstrate willing obedience and a desire to live up to all of the expectations that the Creator would deem necessary.

"By the word of the Lord were the heavens made; and all the hosts of them by the breath of his mouth." *(Psalms 33:6)*

Whether or not the *Creation Category #2*, free-will, moral, *Angelic Hosts* of heaven were created first . . . and if so . . . were created one at a time or en masse', has not yet been determined by this author within the Scriptural accounts. However, Scripture will bear-out that there has been no reproductive permission given within the *Angelic Hosts* constituency. The primary reason for that . . . is that there is no Scriptural evidence of any female angels.

However angelic presence within the existence net of *time* is a Scripturally substantiated fact, and with their creation . . . potentially utilizing the *Basic Creation Element* of Air . . . God has now brought forth an entourage of moral creatures designed to joyfully serve and to minister unto Him.

> *"Praise ye the Lord. Praise ye the Lord from the heavens: praise him in the heights.*
> *Praise ye him, all his angels: praise ye him, all his hosts.*
> *Praise ye him, sun and moon: praise him, all ye stars of light.*
> *Praise him, ye heavens of heavens, and ye waters that be above the heavens.*
> *Let them praise the name of the Lord: for he commanded, and they were created."*
> (Psalms 148:1-5)

God chooses a large habitable planet, within a preferred galaxy, and after their initial orientation, assigns specific angels to initiate construction on the various cities that shall be needed for planetary usage. *(Cities that the angels themselves shall ultimately dwell in, and that future Human Beings that are aborted, or have taken an early bus home, shall be able to dwell in until they eternally decide . . . concerning Christ)* The planet by name is christened Heaven . . . and as the *Third Heaven*, it is actually the second heaven brought forth within creation.

The primary city of importance and recognition on this planet named Heaven is the City New Jerusalem . . . which shall become the dwelling place and headquarters of all of the Universal Operations of Administration, Governance, and Maintenance directed by the Living God.

God further assigns additional angels to record the names of all Adamic-Bloodline Human Beings that shall come forth into existence . . . from the creation of a man named Adam unto the Second Coming of Christ . . . to be preserved within the specifically ordained *Book of Life*. *(Revelation 17:8)*

Additionally, God assigns the other *Books*

that shall be established, to have inscribed within them every name of all members of Humanity that shall come forth into existence during the full Probationary Period for Mankind. And that being accomplished . . . only the blotting out of specific names . . . from either one *Book* or the others remains. *(Revelation 13:8)*

This is a vast universe that we are an active part of . . . and at this point it would behoove us to focus our studies from here-on-in within the parameters of the planet named Earth.

6) The sixth step of ordered creation within the collective net of *time* would be the specific choice of this planet called Earth as the ordained locale where activities of a universal-affecting free-will moral agency nature should transpire.

> **Step A** — Cause that this habitable planet should enjoy the creative delight of the Divine. One of the creation requirements is the formation of an atmosphere or Heaven to surround the planet. This Heaven would become known within *time*

as the *First Heaven* . . . and is the third one to be actually created.

> **"For thus saith the Lord that created the heavens; God himself that formed the earth and made it; he hath established it, he created it not in vain, he formed it to be inhabited: I am the Lord; and there is none else."** *(Isaiah 45:18)*

Step B — Bring forth a *Creation Category #3*, free-will, moral, *Other Creature* constituency to inhabit the planet.

(Scriptural substantiation as to a two-individual genesis with reproductive permission and ensuing increase . . . or of an en masse' creation with no re-production permission . . . is without Scriptural confirmation at this point in time.)

However, Scripture does confirm the reality that they did exist, and that they were intelligent, and that in the process of operating *time*, they formed themselves into nations, and built cities to inhabit. *(Isaiah 14:12 & Jeremiah 4:26)*

Step C — As the inhabitants of Earth are in need of governance . . . and as there is a responsible angel-in-training . . . a marriage of development-perfection and fledgling governance is appropriate. So the angel-in-training named Lucifer is granted a throne, and is set in a position of authority. *(Isaiah 14:13)*

> "... *Thus saith the Lord God; thou sealest up the sum, full of wisdom, and perfect in beauty.*
>
> *Thou hast been in Eden the garden of God; every precious stone was thy covering, the sardius, topaz, and the diamond, the beryl, the onyx, and the jasper, the sapphire, the emerald, and the carbuncle, and gold: the workmanship of thy tabrets and of thy pipes was prepared in thee in the day that thou wast created.*
>
> *Thou art the anointed cherub that covereth; and I have set thee so; thou wast upon the holy mountain of God; thou hast walked up and down in the midst of the stones of fire.*
>
> *Thou wast perfect in thy ways from the day that thou wast created . . .*"
> *(Ezekiel 28:11b-15a)*

Step D — As we are dealing with the free-will moral agency of two different distinct *Creation Category* creatures at the same time, a close eye needs to be kept on all of the current activities occurring upon the planet Earth itself and the extended heavenly influence of the development-perfection candidate named Lucifer.

*(If the **short work** (Romans 9:28) full probationary time allocation for Mankind is a Scripturally calculated 7000 years . . . thought might be given as to the length of the full probationary time allocation for Angelic Hosts and Other Creatures— this author suggests for consideration a full Angelic Probationary time length of 15,000 years or less)*

Step E — Scripture substantiates and records an eruption of rebellion over a period of uncalculated *time*. Free-will, moral agency decides that obeying God was not going to fulfill the purposed Almighty Self exaltation. So the development-perfection candidate named Lucifer, (Isaiah 14:12a) carrying the creative anointing of God, (Ezekiel 28:14a) knowingly, willingly, and consciously, chooses to act contrary to that which he already knows to be right and true *(Ezekiel 28:15)* . . . and in so doing brings the Law of Sin into creative existence and onto the scene.

The reality of Death spills out of the cocoon of Sin and swirls into Three Conditions of devastation. Lucifer becomes the very first captive of that heinous new Law and that Law subsequently drives him unto infectious contact with other free-will moral beings. Unknown numbers of other *Angelic Hosts* and the entire constituency of *Other Creatures* on planet Earth fall prey to his seduction, false promises, and his compulsive quest desires. As they do, they forfeit their own free-will and put on the customized shackles of bondage. *(Romans 6:16)* The condition of Spiritual Death swirls around and engulfs the entire constituency of rebels. And a *last hurrah* final step of deposing the current universal ruler and the ensconcing of himself in the headship position, finally brings a command that severe action be taken. *(Luke 10:18)*

Delayed necessary Judgment will be of no value. Steps must be taken. Decrees are issued . . . travel visas are suspended . . .

catastrophic planetary events occur . . . the swirling condition of Physical Death swallows-up all planetary inhabitants in totality . . . the light of the already existing Sun, and Moon, and Stars is cut off from reaching the planet Earth, and the operational door closes softly as the God of Love sadly leaves the room. *(Psalms 104:6 & Isaiah 14:12-15 & Jeremiah 4:23-26 & Ezekiel 28:15-19 & Matthew 13:35 & II Peter 3:4-7)*

The flooding and lightless conditions affect a freezing of the planet, and nothing survives during the uncalculated *time* expanse of the Ice Age. The dead-in-their-sins unrepentant *Other Creature* inhabitants physically die as a result of the catastrophic occurrences of Psalms 104:6 and Jeremiah 4:23-26, and the wicked disembodied creatures that we know of as *Demons* emerge and become a reality. The animal compliment *dinosaur* contingent on the planet physically dies as well and some of them are preserved within the ice even unto today.

(It is during the period of the Ice Age when God prepares a locale within the interior of planet Earth for the recently judged criminals to reside in throughout the everlasting that lies ahead . . . which shall be referred to in the future as the

Nether World. *(Deuteronomy 32:22 & Matthew 25:41)* *Because we are still dealing with probational necessities there is the possibility of future rebellion and disobedience. Hell will be able to effectively serve all Three contentious Creation Category individuals: Other Creatures . . . Angelic Hosts . . . and Mankind.)*

The Creation of Man

7) The seventh step of ordered creation within the collective net of *time* would be the genesis of an unprecedented moral creation.
>   *(Accurate time calculation is now able to take place for the benefit of Man. Scriptural study shall substantiate this point in time as 4004 B.C.)*

When the Lord returns to the planet Earth . . . the room is dark. Of permissive necessity,

> **"God said, Let there be light: and there was light."** *(Genesis 1:3)*

Clean-up chores are in need of being performed. The room is a judgmental mess and we cannot continue with the new project until we are able to effectively clean it up. So steps must be taken. *(Jeremiah 1:12)*

> **Step 1** — We must re-establish the *First Heaven* atmosphere by separating the waters that are above from the waters that are beneath. *(Genesis 1:6-8)*

Step 2 — The waters beneath then need to be gathered together into one place and labeled as Seas. *(Genesis 1:9-10)*

Step 3 — The dry land that remains is one solid piece and receives the planetary name of Earth. *(Genesis 1:10)*

Step 4 — New grass and other vegetation needs to be brought forth for the benefit of the moral constituency that shall be brought forth. *(Genesis 1:11-12)*

Step 5 — Various adjustments need to be made concerning the already existing Sun, Moon, and Stars whose light was prohibited from reaching the Earth because of Judgment. *(Genesis 1:14-18)*

Step 6 — Living creatures are creatively brought forth utilizing the *Basic Creation Element* of *Water*. Both water-bound creatures such as whales and other fish, and water-fowl creatures that share their arena of survival between the Water and the Air are brought forth. *(Genesis 1:20-22)*

Step 7 — Utilizing the *Basic Creation Element* of *Soil,* living creatures and beasts of the field are creatively brought forth . . . after the creation of a Man named Adam . . . who is responsible for naming the animal compliment of this Probationary Period. *(Genesis 1:24-25 & 2:18-20)*

"And God said, Let us make man in our image, after our likeness: and let them have dominion over the fish of the sea, and over the fowl of the air, and over the cattle, and over all the earth, and over every creeping thing that creepeth upon the earth.

So God created man in his own image, in the image of God created he him; male and female created he them.

And God blessed them, and God said unto them, Be fruitful, and multiply, and replenish the earth, and subdue it: and have dominion over the fish of the sea, and over the fowl of the air, and over every living thing that moveth upon the earth." *(Genesis 1:26-28)*

"And the Lord God formed man of the dust of the ground, and breathed

into his nostrils the breath of life . . ."
(Genesis 2:7a)

Step 8 — We have now reached the juncture of *pièce de résistance* creation. A creature is hand-crafted that far surpasses any moral creation that has been brought forth thus far. This one is of a superior *Creation Category #1* creation. This one is massively authoritative. This one is unprecedented. This one is an Express Image of His Person. *(Hebrews 1:3)* And we will look further at this one within our next study . . . but for right now . . . let us continue in our observation of the Personage of God.

The Personage of The Father

By mutual agreement, the Person that shall occupy the equality position number one within the Trinity shall be known of as the Most High God. *(Genesis 14:18 & Psalms 57:2 & Hebrews 7:1)* That does not equate to that Person or position as being stronger or more powerful than the other two positions . . . it is simply an ascribed title for clarity as to who is who.

The First Person of the Godhead *has* the non-transferable quality of being *Self-Existing* from the everlasting past.

The First Person of the Godhead *has* the non-transferable quality of *Foreknowledge (Isaiah 46:10)* . . . which is the ability of knowing the end of something right from the beginning. *(Which is actually an aspect of Omniscience)*

The First Person of the Godhead *has* the non-transferable quality of Omniscience . . . which is having the ability of knowing all things.

The First Person of the Godhead *has* the non-transferable quality of Omnipotence . . . which is having the ability of being all powerful.

The First Person of the Godhead *has* the non-transferable quality of Omnipresence . . . which is having the ability of making His presence known and felt everywhere at the same time.

The First Person of the Godhead is **not** Omnibody . . . which is having the ability of being bodily everywhere at the same time. That notion is a false doctrine called *Pantheism*. The fact of the matter is that the First Person of the Godhead does not even have a body at all. He has a form *(Philippians 2:8)* and He has a shape *(John 5:37)* . . . but He does *not* have a body . . . Spiritual, *(I Corinthians 15:44b)* Celestial, *(I Corinthians 15:40a)* or Terrestrial. *(I Corinthians 15:40a)*

The spiritual reality is that The First Person of the Godhead is a real Person, with all of the personal limitations that go with it.

In addition, The First Person of the Godhead **is** Light *(I John 1:5b)* . . . and He **is** Love *(I John 4:8b)* . . . and He **is** Life. And in reality who you *is* and what you *has* are two different things . . . even though the statement is grammatically incorrect.

We will find within the Scriptural records that ***The Father*** accomplishes something ***"by"*** or ***"through"*** . . . ***The Son***, and similarly ***"by"*** or ***"through"*** . . . ***The Holy Spirit*** within various contexts. However, within the Scriptures we will not be able to locate any record of something being accomplished ***"by"*** or ***"through"*** ***The Father.*** He holds the supreme operational position of Headship.

Some of the other titles that He specifically carries are: The Creator . . . The Architect of All Things . . . The King of the Kingdom of God . . . The Majesty on High . . . The Father of Glory . . . The Father of Lights . . . and our loving Heavenly Father.

So that we may be better able to recognize Him as we travel through, and drink in, the pages of Scripture:

He is the One who through silent thought gave directives to the Second Person of the Godhead as to what to declare.

He is the One who is 100% God and 0% Humanity.

He is the One who sent the Holy Spirit to *"move upon the face of the waters."* *(Genesis 1:2)*

He is the One who permissively declared concerning light shining once again upon this planet Earth. *(Genesis 1:3)*

He is the One who declared the dividing of the waters above from the waters below. *(Genesis 1:6-7)*

He is the One who directed the grass, and the herb yielding seed, and the fruit yielding tree to come forth. *(Genesis 1:11)*

He is the One who directed the waters to yield forth fishes and fowls, and the Earth to yield forth fowls, beasts of the field, and creeping things. *(Genesis 1:20-25)*

He is the One who, representing the whole of the Trinity, declared that Man should be made **in** the image and **after** the likeness of God. *(Genesis 1:26)*

He is the One who directed the man named Adam and the woman named Eve to multiply before they sinned . . . and to replenish this Earth with intelligent, free-will, moral creatures once again. *(Genesis 1:28)*

He is the One who put the man named Adam within the Garden of Eden to dress it and to keep it. *(Genesis 2:15)*

He is the One who walked with the man named Adam in the cool of the day within the Garden of Eden. *(Genesis 3:8)*

He is the One who gave the man named Adam an opportunity to repent after he had disobeyed His instructions. *(Genesis 3:11)*

He is the One who ordered that a man named Enoch be translated from off of this planet Earth in order to postpone his physical death . . . and for that man to take a walk with Him. *(Genesis 5:24)*

He is the One who declared that the Holy Spirit would not always ***"strive with man"*** but that the man named Adam would be granted 120 more years of physical life in order to change his bad behavior. *(Genesis 6:3)*

He is the One who called a man named Noah to build an ark to the saving of his household. *(Genesis 6:13-14)*

He is the One who directed the man named Noah, and his sons, to multiply after the flood, and to replenish this Earth with intelligent, free-willed men once again. *(Genesis 9:1)*

He is the One, representing the whole of the Trinity that came down to see the city and the tower that men had built. And then led the Trinity to come to the Earth to confound the one language and scatter the people. *(Genesis 11:5 & 7-8)*

He is the One who called an idolatrous man named Abram, and extended to him an offer to enter into a Blood Covenant relationship with Him. *(Genesis 12:1-3 & 17:2)*

He is the One who passed through the pieces of flesh as the *smoking furnace* and established with Himself the original everlasting **Abrahamic Blood Covenant** . . . and the secondarily needed **Christian Blood Covenant.** *(Genesis 15:7)*

He is the One with whom a man named Abraham negotiated concerning the destruction of the cities of Sodom and Gomorrah. *(Genesis 18:23 & 25)*

He is the One who re-confirmed with a man named Isaac; the original Blood Covenant that He had made with a man named Abraham . . . so that the validity of *promise* might become established. *(Genesis 26:3)*

He is the One who re-confirmed for a second time, with his second-born grand-son named Jacob, the original Blood Covenant that He had made with the man named Abraham . . . so that the *purpose of election* reality might become established. *(Genesis 28:13-14)*

He is the One who called a man named Moses to become the deliverer of His people from their physical bondage in a land named Egypt. *(Exodus 3:14-17)*

He is the One who delivered through the man named Moses . . . to only the Israelite people . . . the whole of the Law of Moses, and directed them to observe and obey the *Ten Commandments*. *(Exodus 20:1-17)*

He is the One who delivered through the man named Moses . . . to only the Israelite people . . . an innocent animal, blood-sacrifice atonement system, for the purpose of law-breach-repair. *(Exodus 20:24)*

He is the One who declared that He would raise-up a sanctioned Prophet of God . . . like-unto the man named Moses . . . and directed through the man named Moses that the Israelite people were to receive and hear him. *(Deuteronomy 18:15)*

He is the One who declared . . . and then manifested by the power of the Holy Spirit . . . the kindling of the fires of the Nether World that was **"prepared for the devil and his angels."** *(Deuteronomy 32:22 & Matthew 25:41)*

He is the One who called a man named Joshua to follow in the footsteps of the man named Moses and lead the Israelite people into their promised land. *(Joshua 1:1-3)*

He is the One who raised-up numerous Judges to deliver His Blood Covenant people from bondage . . . from the many years of yielding to sin . . . and the consequences that come forth from disobedience. *(The Book of Joshua)*

He is the One who heard a cry from a woman named Hannah and answered the desire of her heart by bringing forth a man named Samuel the Prophet through her. *(I Samuel 1:11)*

He is the One who told the Prophet named Samuel to hearken unto the voice of the Israelite people in their demand for a king . . . because they chose to reject His leadership. *(I Samuel 8:6-7)*

He is the One who directed the Prophet named Samuel to anoint a man named Saul as the **"captain over his inheritance"** . . . and the man named Saul became the first anointed king of Israel. *(I Samuel 10:1 & 12:1)*

He is the One who repented for making the man named Saul to be the king over His Israelite people. *(I Samuel 15:35)*

He is the One who directed the Prophet named Samuel to anoint the son of a man named Jesse . . . whose son's name was David . . . as the second anointed king over His Israelite people. *(I Samuel 16:1)*

He is the One who within redemptive Trinity operations was going to become **The Father** . . . by written prophetical declaration. *(II Samuel 7:14)(Psalms 89:26)*

Throughout the whole of the written Old Testament . . . it is the First Person of the Godhead who was dealing with the Blood Covenant people that He raised-up through the loins of the one man named Abraham . . . and then through Abraham's son of promise named Isaac . . . and then through Isaac's purpose of election second-born son named Jacob. A nation of people whom He considers Himself to be in a marital covenant with. (Jeremiah 3:14)

In what we know of as the written New Testament, the First Person of the Godhead is still predominate within the Gospel accounts because they are actually Abrahamic Blood Covenant and Mosaic Law accounts, until the last chapters in each account. But . . . there is a transition taking place with the Godhead Persons and their agreed upon responsibilities . . . and the First Person of the Godhead is no longer within the primary focus.

He is the One who through an angel gave direction to a man named Zechariah . . . and informed him of the Prophet that He was going to raise-up through him. *(Luke 1:13-17)*

He is the One who commissioned and directed His Prophet named John the Baptist to reveal unto the Nation of Israel who their promised Messiah was. *(John 1:31-34)*

He is the One who spoke from the *First Heaven* twice to confirm the man named Jesus as His own precious Son. *(Matthew 3:17 & Luke 9:35)*

He is the One who sent the man named Jesus to finish His work within the Nation of Israel . . . concerning His Blood Covenant promises. *(John 4:34)*

He is the One who receives the glory when men acknowledge the man named Jesus for who he is . . . and give the man named Jesus honor. *(John 5:22-23)*

He is the One who graciously draws men unto the man named Jesus Christ of Nazareth . . . that they might be saved from everlasting destruction. *(John 6:44)*

He is the One who sent the man named Jesus . . . and always heard when the man named Jesus prayed . . . and He answered those prayers every time. *(John 11:42)*

He is the One who directed the *Angelic Hosts* to rent the partitioning veil within the holy temple in Jerusalem from the top to the bottom . . . to signify that His promised presence was no longer there in the temple Holy of Holies . . . because of the Israeli people's rejection of the man named Jesus of Nazareth. *(Matthew 27:51)*

He is the One to whom we bring our requests and petitions in prayer . . . utilizing the very name of the risen-from-the-dead man named Jesus. *(Philippians 4:6)*

He is the One who spoke to the Fathers of Israel by the Prophets that He raised-up in days gone by. *(Hebrews 1:1)*

He is the One whose eyes are over the righteous and His ears are open unto their prayers. *(I Peter 3:12)*

He is the One who is seated on a throne in the *Third Heaven* with four and twenty seats around it. *(Revelation 4:2 & 4)*

He is the One who is seated upon a throne with a book in His right hand . . . looking for a man worthy enough to open the book and loose the seals. *(Revelation 5:1-3)*

He is the One . . . by the power of the Holy Spirit . . . who will relocate the city that He built and currently lives in called New Jerusalem . . . to be in close proximity to men for evermore. *(Revelation 21:2-3)*

He is the One who will say **"Behold, I make all things new."** *(Revelation 21:5)*

He is the One . . . along with **The Son** who is the redemptive sacrificial *Lamb of God* . . . that shall be the spiritual temple of the City New Jerusalem. *(Revelation 21:22)*

He is the One who is the Supreme Regent and singular King over the Kingdom of God . . . and He shall remain in His headship position and rule this universe of His for evermore.

The Personage of The Son

By mutual agreement, the Person that shall occupy the equality position number two within the Trinity shall be known of as the Word of God. *(John 1:1 & 14)* He is just as authoritative and powerful as the Most High God who occupies the equality position number one. He willingly submits Himself unto the Most High God as is mutually agreed upon by all Three Members of the Godhead.

The Second Person of the Godhead *has* the non-transferable quality of being *Self-Existing* from the everlasting past.

The Second Person of the Godhead *has* the non-transferable quality of *Foreknowledge* *(Isaiah 46:10)* . . . which is the ability of knowing the end of something right from the beginning. *(Which is actually an aspect of Omniscience.)*

The Second Person of the Godhead *has* the non-transferable quality of Omniscience . . . which is having the ability of knowing all things.

The Second Person of the Godhead *has* the non-transferable quality of Omnipotence . . . which is having the ability of being all powerful.

The Second Person of the Godhead *has* the non-transferable quality of Omnipresence . . . which is having the ability of making His presence known and felt everywhere at the same time.

The Second Person of the Godhead is **not** Omnibody . . . which is having the ability of being bodily everywhere at the same time. That notion is a false doctrine call *Pantheism*. The fact of the matter is that the Second Person of the Godhead, preincarnately, does not even have a body at all. He has a form *(Philippians 2:8)* and He has a shape *(John 5:37)* . . . but He does **not** have a body . . . Spiritual, *(I Corinthians 15:44b)* . . . Celestial, *(I Corinthians 15:40a)* . . . or Terrestrial. *(I Corinthians 15:40a)*

The spiritual reality is that the Second Person of the Godhead is a real Person, with all of the personal limitations that go with it.

In addition, The Second Person of the Godhead **is** Light *(I John 1:5b)* . . . and He **is** Love *(I John 4:8b)* . . . and He **is** Life. And in reality who you **is** and what you *has* are two different things . . . even though the statement is grammatically incorrect.

The Second Person of the Godhead is the **framer** of all things material. The First Person of the Godhead is the **architect** of all of creation . . . and He transfers thoughts unto the Second Person of the Godhead concerning what He desires. The Second Person of the Godhead then decrees declarations of detailed descriptions concerning all *things* that are to be made. He creatively **"calleth those things which be not as though they were:"** *(Romans 4:17b)*

The Second Person of the Godhead is the most identifiable of the Three Persons because of His *"crossover"* from the Realm of the Spirit into the Realm of the Natural and of His becoming a Man.

From the moment of the entrance of the Law of Sin and of Sin's access onto this planet for a second time *(Romans 5:12)* . . . the Realm of the Spirit in which The Personage of God and the *Angelic Hosts* and *Demons* reside has become invisible to the inhabitants of this Earth. *(I Corinthians 13:12a)* The operating Realm of the Spirit has been closed-off from physical sense perception of Human Beings ever since the advent of Spiritual Death . . . but the knowledge of its reality is almost globally known and accepted because of physical results or consequences of actions that have had their origin within the Realm of the Spirit.

> **"For now**, *in this present day*, **we** *spiritually* **see through a glass**, *darkly*. **But then**, *at probation's end*, **face to face.** *Right* **now I know** *only* **in part. But** *when the time comes*, **then shall I know even as also I am known."** *(I Corinthians 13:12)*

"**While** we *purpose to* **look not at the things which are seen,** but at the things which are not seen: for the things which are seen are temporal *and shall pass away*; **but the things which are not seen are eternal** *and shall endure for ever."* *(II Corinthians 4:18)*

Within an enhanced set of verses of I & II Corinthians God reveals unto us this truth.

Because of His ***crossover*** from the Realm of the Spirit into the Realm of the Natural . . . he is the one that we are able to wrap our brains around more readily than the other Two. He is the one Person of the Godhead that we have actually touched. He is an historical individual on this planet. Consider for just a moment:

You are walking down an uneven mountain path toward the gentle lapping of the waves of the sea. The words that you have just heard were spell-binding. And as he spoke, the silence that hung in the air over the thousands that had gathered was discernible. You observe the flow of his movements as he suddenly joins you and matches your pace step for step. The peace that surrounds him is intoxicating. Your mind is flooded with a myriad of thoughts as he glances over and with a soft smile gazes upon your face. What manner of Man is this? continues to arise from within . . . again and again. Suddenly an epiphany bursts upon your consciousness: This is the One who created the very path upon which you travel. This is the One who has brought forth . . . from seemingly nothing . . . the gentle sea that is lapping before you. This is the One who has authored all that your eye can see and your ear can hear. This is the very source of all Life. And yet, he is also a Man . . . just like you.

God desires for all of Mankind to be restored to the position that He originally designed and created them for. In order to keep free-will intact . . . and yet make this restoration possible . . . He has taken on the gifting of becoming a Man Himself . . . and providing for this miraculous restoration through His own death and resurrection.

Some of the titles and names that the Second Person of the Godhead specifically carries in connection with this **"God/Humanity Crossover Project"** are: the Son of God . . . the Advocate . . . the Lamb of God . . . the Resurrection and the Life . . . the Shepherd and Bishop of Souls . . . the Judge . . . the Lord of Lords . . . the Man of Sorrows . . . the Head of the Church . . . Master . . . the Faithful and True Witness . . . the Rock . . . the High Priest of our Confession . . . the Door . . . the Living Water . . . the Bread of Life . . . the Almighty . . . the Rose of Sharon . . . the Alpha and Omega . . . the True Vine . . . the Messiah . . . the Teacher . . . the Holy One . . . the Mediator . . . the Beloved . . . the Branch . . . the Good Shepherd . . .

the Light of the World . . . Shiloh . . . the Image of the Invisible God . . . the Chief Cornerstone . . . the Savior . . . the Author and Finisher of Faith . . . the Everlasting Father of the New Creation . . . the Lion of the Tribe of Judah . . . the I AM . . . the King of Kings . . . the Prince of Peace . . . the Son of Man . . . Prophet . . . the Only Begotten Son . . . the Wonderful Counselor . . . Emmanuel . . . the Bridegroom . . . the Dayspring . . . the Amen . . . the Kings of the Jews . . . Redeemer . . . Anchor . . . the Bright and Morning Star . . . and the Way, the Truth, and the Life.

Following are a number of excerpts from the Scriptures which identify the workings of the Second Person of the Godhead:

He is the One Person of the Godhead who before His incarnation was 100% God and 0% Humanity . . . and after his incarnation is 100% God and 100% Man.

He is the One who within His Divinity receives thought-flow directives from the First Person of the Godhead and utters unalterable detailed descriptions of all things made. *(John 1:3)*

He is the One who is the prophesied **"seed of the woman."** *(Genesis 3:15)*

He is the One who passing through the pieces of flesh as the *burning lamp* . . . established the original everlasting **Abrahamic Blood Covenant** of which Abram was made a part of by faith . . . and also established the secondarily needed **Christian Blood Covenant** with the First Person of the Godhead which will be ratified upon his resurrection from the dead. *(Genesis 15:7)*

He is the One who is the Rock, and is perfect in His work. *(Deuteronomy 32:4)*

He is the One who would become **The Son** by prophetical declaration. *(II Samuel 7:14 & Hebrews 1:5)*

He is the One who would become the Rose of Sharon and the Lily of the Valleys by prophetical declaration. *(Song of Solomon 2:1)*

He is the One who would become the Branch of the Lord . . . by prophetical declaration . . . for those of the Nation of Israel that would escape. *(Isaiah 4:2)*

He is the One who would become the Wonderful Counselor, the Mighty God, the Everlasting Father of the New Creation, and the Prince of Peace by prophetical declaration. *(Isaiah 9:6)*

He is the One who is the Judge and the Lawgiver and the King who will save the Nation of Israel from being destroyed by the Antichrist. *(Isaiah 33:22)*

He is the One who would become the Man of Sorrows acquainted with grief. *(Isaiah 53:3)*

He is the One from whom men would hide their faces. *(Isaiah 53:3)*

He is the One that **The Father** would be pleased to bruise. *(Isaiah 53:10)*

He is the One whose name is the Word. *(John 1:1)*

He is the One who was in the beginning with God. *(John 1:2)*

He is the One in whom was life, and the life was the light of men. *(John 1:4)*

He is the One which lighteth every man that cometh into the world. *(John 1:9)*

He is the One who came unto his own but his own received him not. *(John 1:11)*

He is the One who gives men the power to become the Sons of God . . . even if we simply believe on his name. *(John 1:12)*

He is the One who would become the promised Messiah for the Nation of Israel by prophetical declaration. *(John 4:25-26)*

He is the One unto whom is committed all judgment for Mankind by prophetical declaration. *(John 5:22)*

He is the One who is the resurrection and the life by prophetical declaration. *(John 11:25)*

He is the One who is the Way, the Truth, and the Life by prophetical declaration. *(John 14:6)*

He is the One to whom we **DO NOT** pray . . . but rather present our petitions unto **The Father** in heaven . . . in the name of Jesus. *(John 16:23)*

He is the One who appeared unto the man named Saul of Tarsus after his conversion and told him to leave Jerusalem because the followers of the risen Jesus of Nazareth would not believe nor receive his conversion. *(Acts 22:18)*

He is the One who was made of the ***"Seed of David"*** according to the flesh. *(Romans 1:3)*

He is the One who was declared the Son of God with power by his resurrection from the dead. *(Romans 1:4)*

He is the One who has given grace and apostleship for obedience to the faith. *(Romans 1:5)*

He is the One whom the gospel is all about. *(Romans 1:9)*

He is the One who from before the foundation of the world . . . and by mutual agreement . . . was assigned to be the perfect sacrifice that would be needed to establish a New Law of *"Life in Christ Jesus"* that would override the Law of Sin and the condition of death that came with it. *(Romans 8:2)*

He is the One into whose image men are to be conformed . . . that he might be the first born among many brethren. *(Romans 8:29)*

He is the One who would become a Man Himself . . . and in so doing he would be the *Last Adam* and the *Second Man.* *(I Corinthians 15:45)*

He is the One who would know no sin . . . and yet become Sin . . . that men might be able to become the righteousness of God in him. *(II Corinthians 5:21)*

He is the One who revealed unto the Apostle Paul what was accomplished within the finished work of the cross. *(Galatians 1:12)*

He is the One who was made a curse for us that we might receive the promised blessing of Abraham. *(Galatians 3:13-14)*

He is the One who is the predestined promised **"Seed"** of Abraham. *(Galatians 3:16)*

He is the One by whom we are predestinated unto being the adopted children of the Most High God. *(Ephesians 1:5)*

He is the One with whom we are seated at the right hand of God in heavenly places. *(Ephesians 2:6)*

He is the One by whom we are created to be the workmanship of God. *(Ephesians 2:10)*

He is the One by whom we are brought nigh unto God through his blood. *(Ephesians 2:13)*

He is the One who has broken down the middle wall of partition between the Jew and the Gentile . . . by their living in him. *(Ephesians 2:14)*

He is the One who has abolished the commandments of the Law of Moses by his death upon the cross. *(Ephesians 2:15)*

He is the One who considered it not robbery to be equal with God. *(Philippians 2:6)*

He is the One who would become of no reputation and take upon Himself the form of a servant. *(Philippians 2:7)*

He is the One who found Himself in fashion as a Man, and humbled himself and became obedient unto death. *(Philippians 2:8)*

He is the One who has been given . . . as a man . . . a name which is above every name. *(Philippians 2:9)*

He is the One who is the **First-Born** of every New Creature that comes forth. *(Colossians 1:15)*

He is the One in whom dwelleth all the fullness of the Godhead bodily. *(Colossians 2:9)*

He is the One who has spoiled principalities and powers and made a show of them openly. *(Colossians 2:15)*

He is the One in whom there is no Jew anymore . . . there is no Gentile anymore . . . nor bond nor free. *(Colossians 3:11)*

He is the One who shall descend with a shout . . . with the voice of the Archangel and the trump of God. *(I Thessalonians 4:16)*

He is the One who . . . as a Man . . . is the *Express Image* of the invisible God. *(Hebrews 1:3)*

He is the One who is seated . . . as a Man . . . at the right hand of the First Person of the Godhead who is the Majesty on High. *(Hebrews 1:3)*

He is the One who has inherited a name more excellent than the angels . . . the name of Man. *(Hebrews 1:4)*

He is the One who would taste of Spiritual Death for every man. *(Hebrews 2:9)*

He is the One unto whose eyes all things are naked and open. *(Hebrews 4:13)*

He is the One who has been declared a High Priest forever after the Order of Melchizedek. *(Hebrews 5:10)*

He is the One who would step into a body that was prepared for Him and become flesh. *(Hebrews 10:5)*

He is the One who has begotten us unto a lively hope by his resurrection from the dead. *(I Peter 1:3)*

He is the One who was foreordained before the foundation of the world but was manifest in these last times for us. *(I Peter 1:20)*

He is the One that causes that we, as lively stones, are to be built up as a spiritual house . . . a holy priesthood offering up acceptable spiritual sacrifices unto God. *(I Peter 2:5)*

He is the One who is a stone of stumbling and a rock of offense to those who are disobedient. *(I Peter 2:8)*

He is the One who suffered for us leaving for us an example to follow. *(I Peter 2:21)*

He is the One who bare our sins in his own body on the tree . . . that we being dead to sins should live unto righteousness . . . by whose stripes we were healed. *(I Peter 2:24)*

He is the One who would become the Savior of the world by prophetical declaration. *(I John 4:14)*

He is the One who dictated letters to the Apostle John the Beloved to give unto the seven churches is the land of Asia. *(Revelation – chapters 2 & 3)*

He is the **only** One who was able to take the book out of the right hand of **The Father** sitting upon His throne . . . and open the seals thereof. *(Revelation 5:5)*

He is the One who is called Faithful and True . . . who is sitting on a white horse in the *Third Heaven* when the heaven is opened. *(Revelation 19:11)*

He is the One who is wearing many crowns and

has a name that is written that no man knows. *(Revelation 19:12)*

He is the One with a blood-dripped vesture whose name is called The Word of God. *(Revelation 19:13)*

He is the One who the armies in the *Third Heaven* will follow riding upon other white horses. *(Revelation 19:14)*

He is the One who will rule the nations on planet Earth with a rod of iron. *(Revelation 19:15)*

He is the One who will carry the name KING OF KINGS and LORD OF LORDS. *(Revelation 19:16)*

He is the One who will take the Antichrist and the False Prophet and cast them into the Lake of Fire. *(Revelation 19:20)*

He is the One who slays the remnant of individuals who gathered to make war against him. *(Revelation 19:19 & 21)*

He is the One who sits upon the Great White Throne and from whose face the Earth and heaven flee. *(Revelation 20:11)*

He is the One whose bride . . . the Lamb's wife . . . is the great City New Jerusalem . . . that descends out of the *Third Heaven* from God. *(Revelation 21:10)*

He is the One who along with the Lord God Almighty *(the First Person of the Godhead)* are the temple within the City New Jerusalem. *(Revelation 21:22)*

He is the One who is going to be the very light of the City New Jerusalem. *(Revelation 21:23)*

He is the One who says,

"Behold, I come quickly, and my reward is with me, to give to every man according as his work shall be." *(Revelation 22:12)*

He is the One who says,

"I Jesus have sent mine angel to testify unto you these things in the churches. I am the root and the offspring of David, and the bright and morning star." *(Revelation 22:16)*

He is the One who concluded the written Word of God by declaring, **"Surely I come quickly."** *(Revelation 22:20)*

* * *

The New Creation Jesus of Nazareth is indeed a full one-third of the Divine counsel with all of the powers and characteristics and attributes and qualities and abilities of the other Two Persons . . . within His Divinity. However at the same time he is also 100% Man.

When we study the Word of God and recognize that we are looking at events or situations that are connected with Jesus of Nazareth, we need to discern whether we are observing Jesus from the perspective of His Divinity or from the perspective of his Humanity. Any reference that we may have concerning

Jesus of Nazareth that refers to him as being **made** is referring to his Humanity . . . **nothing** about His Deity was ever made . . . it always was.

*   *   *

As a man Jesus of Nazareth submitted himself wholly unto the God that he worshipped and served . . . the *First Person of the Godhead* who became his Father after his resurrection from the dead. *(II Samuel 7:14)* During his time of ministration here on this Earth, Jesus as the Son of Man received the empowering *cloak* of the *Third Person of the Godhead* who is the Holy Spirit . . . when the Holy Spirit came *upon* him to accomplish every act that we read about within the gospel accounts. *(Luke 3:22)*

It is to our benefit then to identify with what he did as a man . . . a man who was *cloaked* with the Holy Spirit of God for the purpose of benefiting Mankind. Being knowledgeable of what he was doing here on this Earth, the precedent was set by him as a man . . . so that when he was going to return to heaven he could turn right around and tell his disciples,

"Verily, verily, I say unto you, He that believeth on me, the works that I do shall he do also; and greater works than these shall he do; because I go unto my Father." *(John 14:12)*

So . . . what do we see Jesus do as a man:

As a man, he is tempted in the wilderness.

As a man, he turns water into wine at a wedding feast.

As a man, he drives out the thieves and money changers from the temple twice.

As a man, he heals a fellow man of leprosy.

As a man, he calms the wind and the waves of the sea.

As a man, he multiplies the loaves and the fishes.

As a man, he dismisses the demons from the lunatic son, and at Gergasa sends demons into the swine.

As a man, he forgives the sins of a man stricken with palsy.

As a man, he sends Peter down to the seashore to catch a fish and open its mouth and pull out the coin needed to pay the tax.

As a man, he raises up Jairus' daughter from the dead.

As a man virtue flowed forth from him to heal the infirmed woman with the issue of blood.

As a man, he withstands wickedness and unrighteousness from the Pharisees.

As a man, he **suffers** a contradiction of sinners against himself.

As a man, he **suffers** being tempted when he is drawn away of his own lusts.

As a man, he cries out in the Garden of Gethsemane for there to be another way.

As a man, he dies on the cross at Calvary.

As a man, he is raised up from the dead . . . a glorified man to be sure . . . but nevertheless a man.

As a man, he is appointed to be the High Priest forever after the Order of Melchizedek.

As a man, he is seated at the right hand of the Father in heaven today.

As a man, he is in charge of a *work in progress* of subduing all power and all authority.

As a man, he will present unto the Father God in heaven . . . when the work is completed . . . the Kingdom of Heaven of which he is the King.

It is as a man that these and so many more things were done . . . and shall be completed in the days that lie ahead.

The Personage of The Holy Spirit

The *Third Person of the Godhead* is the least understood Person of the Trinity. He is the One who carries the specific title of the Holy Spirit of God. He is the Scripturally demonstrated **_power portion_** of the Godhead.

"And the earth was without form, and void; and darkness was upon the face of the deep. And the SPIRIT OF GOD MOVED UPON THE FACE OF THE WATERS." (Genesis 1:2)

By mutual agreement the Person that shall occupy the equality position number three within the Trinity shall be known of as the Holy Spirit of God.

The Third Person of the Godhead *has* the non-transferable quality of being *Self-Existing* from the everlasting past.

The Third Person of the Godhead *has* the non-transferable quality of *Foreknowledge* (Isaiah 46:10) . . . which is the ability of knowing the end of something right from the beginning. *(And which is actually an aspect of Omniscience)*

The Third Person of the Godhead *has* the non-transferable quality of Omniscience... which is having the ability of knowing all things.

The Third Person of the Godhead *has* the non-transferable quality of Omnipotence... which is having the ability of being all powerful.

The Third Person of the Godhead *has* the non-transferable quality of Omnipresence... which is having the ability of making His presence known and felt everywhere at the same time.

The Third Person of the Godhead is **not** Omnibody... which is having the ability of being bodily everywhere at the same time. That notion is a false doctrine called *Pantheism*. The fact of the matter is that the Third Person of the Godhead does not even have a body at all. He has a form *(Philippians 2:8)* and He has a shape *(John 5:37)*... but He does not have a body... Spiritual, *(I Corinthians 15:44b)* Celestial, *(I Corinthians 15:40a)* or Terrestrial. *(I Corinthians 15:40a)*

The spiritual reality is that The Third Person of the Godhead is a real Person, with all of the personal limitations that go with it.

In addition, The Third Person of the Godhead **is** Light *(I John 1:5b)*... and He **is** Love *(I John 4:8b)*... and He **is** Life. And who you *is* and what you *has* are two different things... even though the statement is grammatically incorrect.

He is the One who is responsible for taking invisible words and invisible faith and making the result of their harmonious union visible. The One who brings into manifestation what has been decreed.

When faith is released He is the One who gives substance to the things that are hoped for. *(Hebrews 11:1)*

He is the One who causes pillars of fire to stand, waters to part, mountains to move, heavens to open, fish to gather, winds to cease, leprosy and other diseases to flee, men to be supernaturally strengthened, flesh to be made whole, bread and fish to multiply, spiritual laws to override natural laws, and every other instance when demonstrated power is seen.

He is the One who is also 100% God and 0% Humanity.

He is the One who imparts *life* unto all of the animated creations that the Godhead has brought forth.

He is the One who took all of the summed-up *Attributes of Transferable Impartation* of the Personage of God and united them with *sinless Dust-Made-Flesh* in the creation of Man.

He is the One who in the fullness of the time *(Galatians 4:4)* took the *Remnant of Sinless Human Flesh* . . . united it with a myriad of *Prophetical Declarations* . . . legally instituted a *New Universal Law* *(Romans 8:2)* and raised-up from the Spiritual and Physical Dead a brand **New Species of Human Creation** that *never* existed before.

He is the foremost figure invisibly, actively, walking through the historical account of the Acts of the Apostles.

He is the One who upon the release of Jesus' faith . . . personally imparts life to, and then takes up residence within . . . every *New Creation* of God and promises to never leave them. *(John 1:12 & 3:3 & 3:5 & II Corinthians 5:17-18)*

He is the One who will remain upon this Earth even after the Church is removed . . . in order to complete the *New Creation, Body-of-Christ Project* that **The Father** has been working on since the resurrection of Christ Jesus. Gifting those who would call upon the name of the Lord in faith unto new life in Christ, throughout the *Time of Jacob's Trouble . . . Daniel's Seventieth Week . . . Tribulation Period.*

Because He is modest He will not talk about Himself. So we are able to learn about Him from what He has recorded concerning creation's history.

Some of the titles and names that He specifically carries and can be identified by are: the Spirit of Truth . . . the Spirit of Adoption . . . the Seven Spirits of God . . . the Comforter . . . the Spirit of Grace . . . and the Spirit of the Lord.

He is the One who through faith brought forth into existence all things . . . and manifested *life* where it was ordained concerning the decrees made by the *Second Person of the Godhead* which had been directed by the *First Person of the Godhead* in line with their agreed upon positions and responsibilities.

Scripturally speaking:

He is the One who brooded over the water . . . waiting for the command from the *First Person of the Godhead*. *(Genesis 1:2)*

He is the One who "***hastened***" *(Jeremiah 1:12)* the declaration spoken to disperse the chaos and allow the light from the already existing Sun, Moon, and Stars to once again shine upon this planet Earth. *(Genesis 1:3)*

He is the One who "***hastened***" *(Psalms 147:15 & Jeremiah 1:12)* the declarations spoken to divide the waters above from the waters below and cause a firmament to become manifest. *(Genesis 1:6-7)*

He is the One who "***hastened***" *(Psalms 147:15 & Jeremiah 1:12)* the declarations spoken to gather the waters below together into one place. *(Genesis 1:9)*

He is the One who "***hastened***" *(Psalms 147:15 & Jeremiah 1:12)* the declarations spoken to bring forth grass and the herb yielding seed and the tree yielding fruit. *(Genesis 1:12)*

He is the One who took the *Basic Creation Element* of *Water* and "***hastened***" *(Psalms 147:15 & Jeremiah)* the declarations spoken and brought forth and imparted animated *life* into whales and every living creature which the waters would produce. *(Genesis 1:21)*

He is the One who took the *Basic Creation Element* of *Soil* **(Earth or Dust)** and **"hastened"** *(Psalms 147:15 & Jeremiah 1:12)* the declarations spoken and brought forth and imparted animated *Life* unto all that the dust would produce. *(Genesis 1:24)*

He is the One who took the *Basic Creation Element* of *Soil* and fused that element with Divine Image . . . imparting eternal *Life* into the flesh-body-*likeness* of God that was brought forth from that *Soil*. *(Genesis 2:7)*

He is the One who **"hastened"** *(Psalms 147:15 & Jeremiah 1:12)* the declarations spoken to cause to grow every tree that is pleasant to the sight and good for food within the Garden of Eden that God Himself planted. *(Genesis 2:8-9)*

He is the One who took the sinless flesh-body-*likeness* element of God and fused that element with Divine Image . . . imparting *Life* into the female-compliment-*likeness* of God that was brought forth from the Man named Adam. *(Genesis 2:22)*

He is the One who would anoint men or women by coming *upon* them or empowering them to accomplish specific tasks that the *First Person of the Godhead* would have for them to do throughout the Old Testament.

* * *

He is the One who acted upon the Law of Agreement *(Matthew 18:19)* when a virgin girl named Mary submitted herself to whatever God desired to use her for. And the Holy Spirit of God caused a conception to occur within the virgin's womb without the benefit of a Human male in order to initiate the preparation of the sinless body for the *Second Person of the Godhead* to incarnate into. *(Luke 1:35 & 38 & Hebrews 10:5)*

* * *

He is the One who temporarily filled a woman named Elizabeth and caused the babe that was in her womb to leap at the salutation of a woman named Mary. *(Luke 1:41)*

He is the One who revealed to a twelve-year old boy named Jesus of Nazareth . . . using a Word of Knowledge *(I Corinthians 12:8)* . . . while he was at a Passover celebration . . . that he was in reality the *Second Person of the Godhead.* *(Luke 2:49 & Philippians 2:8)*

He is the One who directed the man named Jesus of Nazareth to leave the city of Nazareth and go down South to the Jordan River in order to be water baptized by a man named John. *(Matthew 3:13)*

He is the One who came *upon* the man named Jesus of Nazareth in the form of a dove at the Jordan River to empower him to do what he needed to do in ministering to men here on this Earth. *(Matthew 3:13 & Mark 1:10)*

He is the One against whom blasphemy **shall not** be forgiven in this world or in the world to come. *(Matthew 12:31-32)*

He is the One who is the *other* **comforter** that the man named Jesus of Nazareth said that he would ask **The Father** to send. *(John 14:16)*

He is the One who is the Spirit of Truth. *(John 14:17)*

He is the One who will bring back to our remembrance the things that our God has said. *(John 14:26)*

He is the One who will not speak of Himself. *(John 16:13)*

He is the One who gives unto us power after that He comes *upon* us like a *cloak*. *(Acts 1:8)*

He is the One who caused the sound as of a rushing mighty wind and appeared as cloven tongues of fire upon the gathered disciples on the Day of Pentecost. *(Acts 2:2-3)*

He is the One who gave men utterance and caused that every gathered man should hear the praises of God in their own native tongues. *(Acts 2:6)*

He is the One who gives boldness unto *New Creations* and gives them what they need to speak in that hour. *(Acts 4:8-12)*

He is the One who translated a man named Philip from being at a river that was in the area of Gaza unto the city of Azotus which was about twenty-five miles away. *(Acts 8:39-40)*

He is the One who came upon a man named Cornelius and other Gentiles when they heard the Word of God preached and believed in their heart unto righteousness. *(Acts 10:44-45)*

He is the One who declared the man named Jesus of Nazareth to be the Son of God with anointing power by raising Jesus up from the Spiritual and Physical Dead. *(Romans 1:4)*

He is the One who is the Spirit of Adoption by which we are made the sons and daughters of God. *(Romans 8:15)*

He is the One who helps our infirmities by making intercession through us with groaning which cannot be uttered. *(Romans 8:26)*

He is the One who ultimately will conform us into the very image of Christ Jesus our Lord. *(Romans 8:29)*

He is the One who will give unto us supernatural giftings as He wills. *(I Corinthians 12:11)*

He is the One who births individuals unto new spirit *life* and then seals those individuals within their recreated spirits when they have received the gift of God. *(Ephesians 1:13)*

He is the One through whom we have access unto **The Father.** *(Ephesians 2:18)*

He is the One that we should not grieve. *(Ephesians 4:30)*

He is the One who makes us lively stones that together we may make up a spiritual habitation for the Lord. *(I Peter 2:5)*

He is the One who is the **seed** spoken of by the Apostle John that causes that a man cannot sin in his born-again, recreated, human spirit anymore. *(I John 3:9)*

He is the One by whom we know that we dwell in God and that God dwells in us. *(I John 4:13)*

He is the One who bears witness of what God has done through the finished work of Jesus Christ within the Plan of Redemption for Mankind. He is the Spirit of Truth. *(I John 5:6)*

He is the One who has given unto us a prayer language by which we may build up our faith. *(Jude 20)*

Permanent residents of God's City New Jerusalem will be **The Father, The Son, The Holy Spirit,** and all of the <u>New Creation</u> children of the Most High God.

Only these particular Human men and women who are born-again and become *New Creatures*, and are the sons and daughters of the Most High God will reside within the City New Jerusalem and have the blessing of the *Third Person of the Godhead* living within their being forever more.

And for all of eternity only Immortal children of the Most High God will be directed and empowered in all that they may do by the Holy Spirit of God Himself.

It has been our delight to walk through the adventureland of creation with you. We pray that you have received insight and encouragement. We also pray that this trip has caused you to redouble your efforts concerning the study of the Word of God. Remember, the risen Lord of Glory will return soon. Make sure you are ready.

Maranantha!

Meet the Author

By-The-Book Ministries, Inc. began in 2001 as a teaching outreach. Rob E. Daley has been gifted by God to be able to explain biblical truths in an easy to understand manner.

Many have been blessed by his teaching style.

Rob was saved and filled with the Holy Spirit in 1978 and has been instructed by the greatest teacher of all—the Spirit of Truth Himself. Rob is an ordained minister with the Assemblies of God International Fellowship and has pastored in various churches over the past 34 years.

It is the desire of this ministry to see the body of Christ solidly taught, and grow up into the things of the Lord. Rob is available for seminars, retreats, conventions, etc.

Rob can be reached at:

thedaleys@bythebookministries.org

http://robdaleyauthor.com

www.ingramcontent.com/pod-product-compliance
Lightning Source LLC
Chambersburg PA
CBHW032207040426
42449CB00005B/479